CHIC STAYS

CONDÉ NAST TRAVELLER'S
FAVOURITE PEOPLE ON THEIR FAVOURITE PLACES

Back cover: An aerial view of the Maldives. © Jenny Zarins, Condé Nast Traveller Ltd.

3 Park Avenue, 27th Floor
New York, NY 10016 USA
Tel.: 212-989-6769 Fax: 212-647-0005
www.assouline.com
ISBN: 9781614285373
10 9 8 7 6 5 4 3 2

Art director: Jihyun Kim and Camille Dubois
Editorial director: Esther Kremer
Editor: Lindsey Tulloch
Printed in China.
Color separation by Altaimage.

Condé Nast Traveller

CHIC STAYS

CONDÉ NAST TRAVELLER'S FAVOURITE PEOPLE ON THEIR FAVOURITE PLACES

ASSOULINE

CONTENTS

INTRODUCTION

The first hotel I remember staying at was the Cala di Volpe, in Sardinia. It was the early 1980s. The sea clinked like diamonds, the air smelt of Coppertone, Van Cleef & Arpels's First, good times and gin. The men unfolded on their sun loungers with sizzling belly laughs like the world was ripe, and all the girls, brown as toffee, wandered around without their bikini tops, twisting their necklaces like words. It was here that a waiter taught me how to peel a peach in one piece. Massaging just so, on a slow rotation, scalping its fuzziness - ta-da! Later, there would be other holidays and other hotels. The Ritz-Carlton in Boston, where even the sand in the ashtrays was imprinted with its imperial-looking insignia. Woody Allen - *Woody Allen!* - toot-tooting on his clarinet in the café at the Carlyle, just like they said he would! Le Royal on the grand avenue of Deauville, all silver cloches and chocolate mousse and watching the raindrops consume themselves down the windowpanes of the empty summer dining room. Then, of course, there was also the hut on the tiny island of Roatán, in Honduras, surrounded by pigs who've escaped from their sty, and a sleepless night crushing cockroaches with the complete works of Dickens. But then, also, the joy of Le Bristol, a cacophony of chintz and clickety-clackety floors, taking baths in the middle of the day and reading novels while looking out at the leaden rooftops of Paris. The fun of Charlotte Street in Fitzrovia and its honesty bars: too drunk to sleep, too drunk not to be honest. Hotels checked in and out of, with sleep and without. Hotels as refuge and rapture. Hotels as a timeline on which all our adventures are punctuated, as smart and neat as life's little commas and full stops. For what are hotels if not celebrations of the time lived, as well as the times lived in? Here in this book, our favourite people write love letters to these particular pockets of delight.

MELINDA STEVENS
EDITOR, *CONDÉ NAST TRAVELLER UK*

FIONA KERR: COMMISSIONING EDITOR MATTHEW BUCK: PHOTOGRAPHIC EDITOR
TABITHA JOYCE: EDITORIAL ASSISTANT

EDDIE REDMAYNE

LE SIRENUSE

The first time my wife, Hannah, and I stayed at Le Sirenuse, our minds were blown. We were spending a week or two on the Amalfi Coast to attend the Giffoni Film Festival, and many friends had suggested that we visit this gem of a hotel. You'll find that when people speak about Le Sirenuse, it tends to be in quite breathless tones. It is the family hotel of Antonio Sersale - his grandfather was one of four Neapolitan siblings who turned their summer house into a hotel back in 1951 - who now runs it with his wife, Carla. His reputation precedes him: his effervescent ebullience, his warmth, his kindness.

Le Sirenuse is set up at the top of Positano like a clam clutching onto the rock. It has the most formidable restaurant, but when we arrived, Hannah and I had been fantasising about the simplest of dishes: pasta, caprese salad and a cold glass of white wine. They made us this, off menu, and that dream of simplicity was exactly what came. It couldn't have been more delicious, eaten on the terrace overlooking that beautiful coast. My shoulders dropped by about five centimetres in that moment.

In all the rooms there's a little book beside the bed containing an article written by John Steinbeck when he stayed in 1953. Reading it, you can feel the embedded history of the place, the romance of the story of the Sirens and the overwhelming seduction of this part of the world. There's an intimacy to Le Sirenuse, a wonderful quietness. There's this one window that frames the town's Duomo with its coloured tin-tiled roof, and it looks just like a painting.

But do see if you can get in Antonio's good books and grab a moment on the hotel's vintage Riva. Step down past the little Duomo and onto the most beautiful boat, which putters off past the tiny Li Galli islands, once owned by the director Franco Zeffirelli. Then head out into the middle of nowhere, drop anchor and take a dive into the azure sea. The water feels too blue for Europe - even a colour-blind person like me can see the vividness. And then Antonio serves Piscines: Champagne over ice. That's one of the most blissful memories I have.

Sirene
ANTE - BAR TEL 089.875.490
RISTORANTE "DA ADOLFO" 089.875022

11
21
22
24
25
26
27
32
33
34
35
36
37
38
46
47
48
49
54
55
56

"The first time my wife and I stayed at Le Sirenuse, our minds were blown. You'll find that when people speak about the hotel, it tends to be in quite breathless tones."

JASON WU

HOTEL ESENCIA

Hotel Esencia really feels like a sanctuary. The first time I visited, I arrived at night and was led through these winding, narrow paths to the main whitewashed villa, once the holiday home of an Italian duchess. It really lends itself to the idea of still being that home away from home, which is often easier said than done. The owner, Kevin Wendle, has become a close friend: He has impeccable taste and is one of the most generous hosts I know. On that first trip he gave me a suite on one of the top floors in the house, which is all glass with 360-degree views; there are also little cottages tucked around the surrounding gardens. I woke up that first morning to see the beach, the trees, the lush scenery. It was so incredible to wake up in the middle of all that beauty, when I'm used to waking up in New York City, where it is buildings, buildings, buildings, all skyscrapers and traffic.

I'm not a beach shack person, and Hotel Esencia is a much more sophisticated spot on the sand. Everything is very refined: the decor, with mid-century furniture and curated art; the food, lots of ceviche and delicious avocado fries; even the tequila. I discovered one brand on my last trip to Hotel Esencia called Casa Dragones, which is so smooth that you sip it from a Champagne flute.

When I'm here, I hardly leave the hotel. This is a place where you just let the day pass, drifting from breakfast to the beach, from lunch to the pool to the spa. When I leave I stock up on the local oil they use. I love to draw on the beach, and I always take my sketchbook with me - if you look at my resort 2016 lookbook, you can see how Hotel Esencia inspired me, right down to the decor. Sometimes to really design, you need there to be nothing crazy going on around you, and Hotel Esencia is exactly where you'll find that pocket of perfect peace.

LANVIN
MONDINO
BOTERO
CIRCUS
EDWARD HOPPER
SALADINO VILLA
Van Gogh
Jean-Michel Basquiat
MALEVICH
SUPREMATISM
MANOR HOUSES IN NORMANDY
LA CÔTE D'AZUR
PICASSO
RICHARD AVEDON PORTRAITS
Walker Evans
WILLIAM WEGMAN PUPPIES
Scavullo
Intérieurs de Provence
Monet
The Jean-Michel Basquiat
LA MAISON DE VERRE
Made by Indians
THE ARCHITECTS HOME
CY TWOMBLY DRAWINGS
Bob Dylan
MAISONS RURALES ET VERNACULAIRES EN PROVENCE
RUSCHA
RUSCHA
RUSCHA
LE STYLE PUTMAN
BIRTH OF THE COOL
CENTURY
FERMIN REVUELTAS
THE SHAKERS
CY TWOMBLY
ANNIE LEIBOVITZ
VANITY FAIR'S HOLLYWOOD
TASCHEN
NEW YORK
THE AMERICANS
KAPOOR
Robert Smithson Spiral Jetty
A TOUCH OF STYLE
CARLOS MOTA
CALIFORNIA DESIGN
Wolfgang Tillmans

KATE WINSLET

EILEAN SHONA

Luxury. Some of us are comforted by that word, some of us are deeply panicked by it, and others live in the hope of one day finding it. However, the majority of people I know are enthralled by the idea of luxury well earned at the end of an adventure-filled day and the uncertainty of the wild outdoors - the perfect combination of which can be found on Eilean Shona's magnificent isolated shores.

A spectacularly beautiful isle on the west coast of Scotland, from which Eigg, Muck and Rum can be seen in the distance like giant sea myths emerging from below, it has been owned and loved by Vanessa Branson and Robert Devereux for more than two decades. Their friends, children and children's friends have filled every crack and peak with memories over the years, the presence of which can be keenly felt as you wander through magical Peter Pan forests and throw yourself against wild winds on remote white-sand beaches. This is the kind of magic one longs for, looks for and seldom finds.

To reach it, leave your car behind on the mainland and hop aboard the island boat, for there are no roads on Shona. There are a few tracks here and there, but be prepared to carve your own pathways to adventure. Will those be from the main house or from one of the six cottages? Or why not take the whole island for yourself? With all the wisdom of Vanessa and Robert's vast travels thrown in for good measure, Shona has one foot in today's culture and the other firmly rooted in a mystical past. Modern art mixes with old, and Moroccan plates and rugs adorn cupboards and floorboards of the recently renovated Old Schoolhouse, from where I write this. All I can hear is the sound of an excitable stream, babbling down the hillside to the loch, and the wind whipping gently through the valley. A faint pop and creak comes from the wood-burning stove in the corner of the whitewashed kitchen, upon which we just fried up some fish. And if I were to describe the cauldrons of mussels we cooked on the beach, washed down with Chablis we chilled in the sea, you probably wouldn't believe me.

So if you feel the need for extreme peace, look no further. If you long to look at your mobile phone and see that it constantly says NO SERVICE, this is the sanctuary you have been searching for. Eilean Shona is heaven on earth.

Acharacle, Argyll, Scotland *eileanshona.com*

NO
WELLIES
INSIDE

"Hop aboard the island boat,
for there are no roads on Shona.
There are a few tracks here and there,
but be prepared to carve your own
pathways to adventure."

SOFIA COPPOLA

PALAZZO MARGHERITA

There's a certain parallel between directing a film and creating a hotel. I think that's why my father is so good at making hotels: He knows that they have a story and how to create an atmosphere; he has that director's eye for detail.

Palazzo Margherita is an old noble family's house, built in 1892, in the very south of Italy. It sits on a square in the town of Bernalda, a little Eden behind these huge wooden doors. My great-grandfather moved from the town to New York over a century ago, and it still feels like Italy from another era, with grandmas' laundry hanging from balconies and old men sitting on the sidewalk all day.

Slip off the street, through the gates and into the gardens, and Palazzo Margherita is its own magical world. I could sit in the courtyard all day or with a book by the pool, where the wonderful staff bring platters of fresh fruit - plums, apricots - on crushed ice. In the summer, when it gets really hot, I wander into the kitchen and feast on incredible pasta or a salad of fresh tuna, handfuls of rocket and fine red onions, served on beautiful, hand-painted blue-and-white dishes that my mother chose from a nearby town. Then I pull up a seat at the Cinecittà Bar, named after the legendary Italian movie studio, and drink iced coffee while the jukebox plays old tunes, or wander into town for gelato at Gelateria Novecento.

I love to stay in suite four, my room, all pretty pinks and greys, with a balcony overlooking the courtyard and a claw-foot tub in the bathroom. Every room in the palazzo has its own personality. The architect, Jacques Grange, restored a lot of original details: beautiful murals, intricate tiling and frescoes on the ceilings. And upstairs, there's a big salon with a movie screen, where my father has put the whole Martin Scorsese collection of the history of Italian cinema in the library. I remember one time watching a comedy called *Sedotta e Abbandonata* (*Seduced and Abandoned*) from 1964. There's something very romantic about these old Italian films, in this old Italian house - it makes you feel like you've stepped into another life.

COPPOLA
Tavoularis
4 JUILLET 2010

SEBASTIAN FAULKS

CEYLON TEA TRAILS

Sri Lanka wasn't always a tea island. Until 1870, the hills were covered in coffee plants. Almost overnight, a fungus wiped out every bush and took away the livelihoods of thousands. Nothing daunted, the planters, led by an Englishman named James Taylor, started to import tea plants from China and India. Within a decade, Ceylon, as it was then, forgot coffee and became one of the world's leading exporters of Broken Orange Pekoe, English Breakfast and all the other varieties of this durable and easy-going plant. 'The tea fields of Ceylon are as true a monument to courage as is the lion at Waterloo,' said Sir Arthur Conan Doyle when he considered this response to adversity.

I first visited Sri Lanka in 1981, when I was part of the *Guardian* newspaper cricket team. Every single man in that bunch of dreamers, cranks and prima donnas fell in love with the place. Up in the tea country, at Nuwara Eliya, we stayed at the Hill Club. It was like a boarding house in postwar Bexhill - on the bedside table was an AA gazetteer from 1952. You had to wear a tie in the dining room, and the dignified white-coated Sinhalese butler was called Andrews, a name he had inherited from a previous retainer.

I was back in tea country recently with my wife, in the nearby plantations of Bogawantalawa, which radiate from a huge reservoir. You can stay overnight in four of the old planters' bungalows, which together comprise the Tea Trails hotel, brought up to date but still giving a good sense of what the colonial life must have felt like. Pretty good, I'd say. We stayed in Castlereagh, a bungalow on the water, and in Tientsin, higher in the hills, named after a Chinese tea village. Tientsin has the more authentic planter feel, but Castlereagh the shimmering lake view. A hundred years ago, you might have grown bored if you were upcountry for more than a few months, itching for a bit of Colombo nightlife. But for a visitor today, the combination of long vistas, bright light and local food is irresistible.

ERDEM MORALIOGLU

PARK HYATT TOKYO

I've always been fascinated by Japan - the people, the history, the food, everything. I think there is something so wonderfully otherworldly about it. There's always something new to discover in Tokyo: On my last trip, we had an incredible meal at Shirube, a completely unassuming *izakaya* tucked behind the train tracks with sensational blowtorch-grilled mackerel. I also loved Bar Martha in Ebisu, which has the most amazing vinyl record collection lining the walls.

Yet the Park Hyatt Tokyo doesn't change. And that's exactly the appeal - it's not conceptual, it's not high design, nor is it overly heritage. It's not desperately trying to define itself in the way new hotels seem to do these days. Instead of focussing on highlighting the hotel inwardly, it highlights its location - the city, the Tokyo skyline, which is one of the most distinct in the world. The first thing I do when I stay is throw myself into the pool to swim away the jet lag. It's on the forty-seventh floor, and you can see all the way out to snowy Mount Fuji on a clear day. There's a wonderful sense of calm throughout the whole hotel, but especially here swimming laps high up in the sky - yet you are looking out over one of the busiest, fastest-moving cities on earth. It's a powerful contrast.

In a way, the hotel has been immortalised in *Lost in Translation*. I love that film, and the famous scene where Bill Murray sits alone at the New York Bar drinking seventeen-year-old Hibiki whisky has stuck with me. The last time I was at that bar, it was Christmas Eve. There was a classic big band and singer playing American jazz hits, and I had a Wagyu beef burger with a dirty martini while Tokyo twinkled in the distance. That, in a way, sums up the Park Hyatt's charm: the timeless formality, the incredible views and the slight incongruousness of it all. It's graceful, unassuming and iconic - and I love it.

LUMINE1
LABI

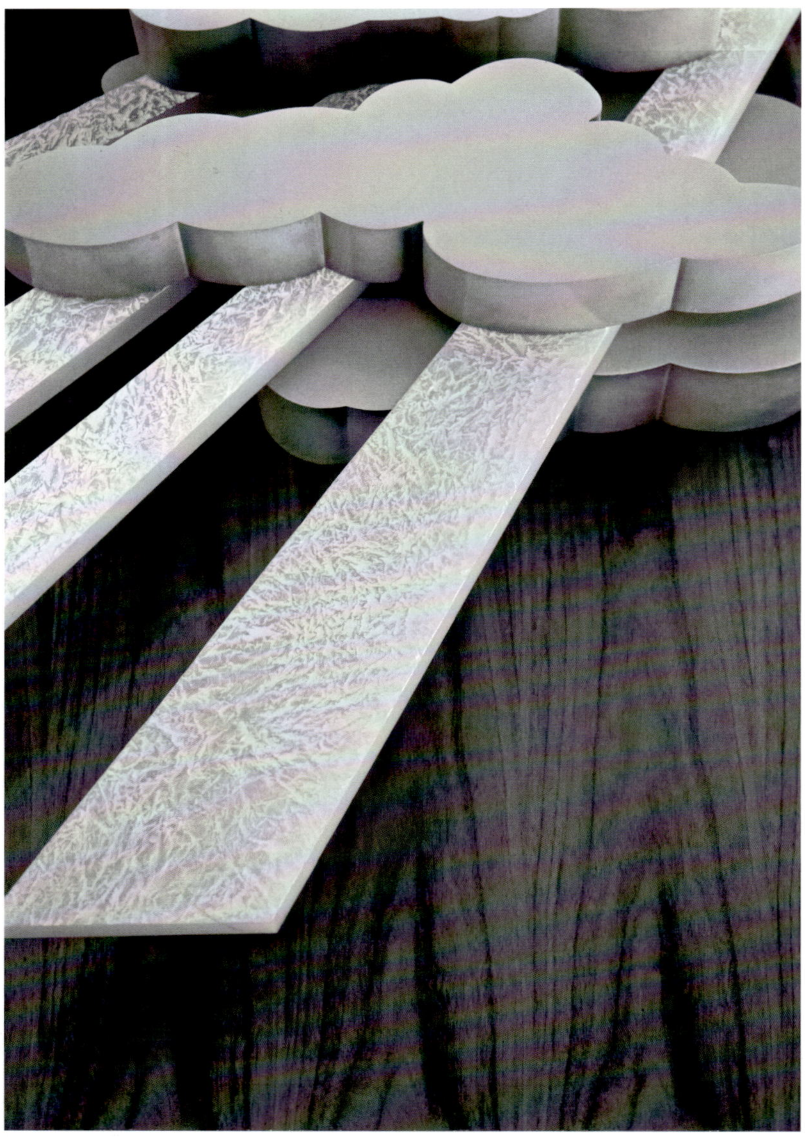

L'ATTORE
VISCONTI

"There's a wonderful sense of calm throughout the hotel, but especially here swimming laps high up in the sky - yet you are looking out over one of the busiest, fastest-moving cities on earth."

ALESSANDRA AMBROSIO

UXUA CASA HOTEL & SPA

All my friends told me that UXUA is the most beautiful place to stay in Trancoso. It's right at the centre of the old town, next to the picturesque square, the Quadrado. The whole region of Bahia is exactly what I expected it to be: quaint, authentic and filled with culture. Trancoso itself is a small village just like where I grew up in the south of Brazil. It seems almost stuck in the past, which for me is so special. Bossa nova music floats through the air, the food is unbelievable, made from superfresh ingredients, and there's always a little party going on somewhere.

What's really unique about UXUA is that it's made up of lots of little *casas*, and each is completely different, but all have a rustic beach vibe. One, Casa da Árvore, is a tree house - which my kids love - spread over three floors straddling the branches of a jackfruit tree and a cinnamon tree, with a swing seat hanging beneath it. If you're a couple, however, I think the perfect room is a traditional aqua-painted house called Gulab Mahal, which faces the square. I love just lounging around, looking out the window, watching and listening to life on the Quadrado: guys playing guitars and people singing old Brazilian songs, children running about in front of one of the prettiest and oldest churches in Brazil.

Gorgeous UXUA's beach bar, fashioned from an old fisherman's boat, is deeply relaxing and only a five-minute stroll from the hotel. I love drinking the most amazing pineapple-and-ginger caipirinhas here and watching other guests learning capoeira on the deserted beach while my kids splash around where the river meets the ocean.

“I love drinking the most amazing pineapple-and-ginger caipirinhas here and watching people learning capoeira on the deserted beach.”

BILL NIGHY

THE CARLYLE

New York City is a theatre town. I always seem to be working here, which is such a marvellous way to see the city - you really become part of the language of a place rather than just swinging by. The first time I did a play in New York it was Christmas, and people kept telling me how cold it was going to get. Being from London, I was very sniffy. And then it got cold - it got really cold. It's a wonderful time to be here but nothing beats New York in the spring. On a crisp spring day that skyline is the most exciting in the world.

For me, the Carlyle is a specific expression of New York City and the only place to stay. I don't really feel comfortable in a lot of the modern hotels; they seem to get things wrong in terms of aesthetic. But the Carlyle has a sense of history. It's elegant and attractive without being over the top. I can't help but think of JFK and Marilyn Monroe and Frank Sinatra singing something like 'The Very Thought of You'. It transports me to the 1940s, when everybody dressed so well. Things seem to have gone downhill since then, but the Carlyle remains.

I always stay in Suite 1103, which is the best way to arrive in New York. It's spectacular in its quiet way, with thick carpets, an enormous comfy bed and a living room I could actually see myself living in. Most of all I like the fact that there's a piano in Bemelmans Bar. Not that I play the piano - I just like living with one. There's a very sweet little room right next to the bar called the Gallery. I leave the bar to younger men and have a soda water in there. I might go crazy and have a burger too, but without the bun, which is all very rock 'n' roll.

In the morning all I need is an espresso and scrambled eggs. I'll take a stroll one block to Central Park. Then I'll find a good bookshop because there isn't a nicer way to spend a day in New York.

The Carlyle

ESSEX
HOUSE

LETTERS
THE CUTLER MAIL CHUTE CO.
LETTER·BOX
U·S·MAIL
CUTLER MAIL CHUTE CO.
ROCHESTER, N.Y.

GANCIA
VERMOUTH BIANCO

SIR ROGER MOORE

LA COLOMBE D'OR

It's impossible to say how many times my wife, Kristina, and I have dined and stayed at La Colombe d'Or over the years - too many to count. Since about 1995, we've been going there to eat on an almost weekly basis in the summer months. We even stay at the hotel for our holidays, decamping for two or three weeks at a time, although it's only 40 kilometres away from our home in Monaco. We love it more than anywhere else in the world.

By now, we've checked in to every room of the hotel - those by the pool, where a giant Calder mobile dances in the breeze, and those looking out over the village. It's impossible to choose a favourite: They all have character and, charmingly, are not ultramodern, yet they have everything you could possibly need.

It's the Roux family who are the most important part of La Colombe d'Or - they opened it as a hotel in 1920, and it's now in its third generation. I can't imagine it without them and their wonderful staff. Their art collection is quite extraordinary too; the hotel was a regular haunt of modernists, including Picasso and Chagall. Our favourite piece is the ceramic mural that graces the terrace, by Fernand Léger.

For many years we lived in Saint-Paul-de-Vence, above the village, and La Colombe d'Or was our local restaurant. The menu has always stayed pretty much the same, but why change? The platter of hors d'oeuvres - a splendid mixture of starters served on a seemingly endless procession of little white dishes - is famous, and there is also the most wonderful soufflé. You don't have to wait forty minutes for it either!

Our preferred spot, however, is at the bar. To sit with a drink and some olives and nuts, watching the villagers and tourists go by, is quite delightful and relaxing. And this is not just any world: La Colombe d'Or is one of the best places for star-gazing, particularly at Cannes Film Festival time. Today you might spot Michael Caine, Bill Wyman, Elton John, Donald Sutherland, Sean Connery, David Beckham or Joan Collins; we used to see Michael Winner, Christopher Lee and Donald Pleasence here often. It's quite magical.

HANS HEDBERG
1994

"The menu has always stayed pretty much the same, but why change?"

La COLOMBE d'

LIVIA FIRTH

SONG SAA

Song Saa means 'the sweethearts', and the story of it is a rare tale of love over greed. When Melita Hunter and her husband, Rory, first discovered this pair of islands in the untouched Koh Rong archipelago, they fell in love with the place and immediately vowed to protect it. With their Song Saa Foundation, they created the first-ever marine reserve in Cambodia. They have involved the local community from the start, and it's truly a model sustainable business.

Colin and I have been lucky enough to stay in wonderful hotels around the world. But the true soul of Song Saa makes it different from other places. Melita and Rory describe it as luxury that treads lightly, and it's a lovely way of putting it. Real luxury today should be all about integration. Everything here has been produced with local materials and recycled and upcycled when possible.

The rooms are so private and beautiful that you are tempted to never leave your cocoon and instead just languish in the pool overlooking the sea. But when you emerge, the people who run the hotel immediately feel like family. You want to spend time with them, listening to their stories.

One day we took part in a very special Buddhist blessing ceremony and, a few months later, I'm still grateful to wear the red string they put round my wrist. All the meals on the island are, well, spectacular. Each night at a different location: a table on the beach; another under a tree, with millions of tea lights; even a feast in the middle of the pool. The spa also offers unforgettable rituals. Under a pagoda on the sea, all you hear is the water and the birds in the trees.

There is an Italian expression, 'mal d'Africa', or 'Africa sickness', used to describe the longing you feel for Africa once you leave it. Well, the day we left Song Saa, hugging and kissing everyone, we knew we had 'mal di Song Saa'. We long to be back there.

LUKE EVANS

SOHO HOUSE ISTANBUL

Istanbul is a city that buzzes with energy. The streets are narrow and the drivers seem to have some insane sense of bravery - how many of the cars have wing mirrors left, I don't know. It's astonishingly beautiful, too. There are so many iconic buildings on both sides of the Bosphorus, from the Hagia Sophia with its stunning mosaics to the strangely peaceful yet imposing Basilica Cistern with its resident koi carp swimming around in the dark waters; from the magnificent, sprawling Topkapi Palace to the Grand Bazaar, a glorious labyrinth of stalls teeming with colour, light, texture and scents. My tip: Go with an empty suitcase and fill it with intricate coloured-glass lampshades, beautiful painted plates and Turkish delight that comes in so many flavours, half of which I didn't even know existed.

In the middle of this crazy city, Soho House Istanbul is like an oasis. You arrive down a quiet street in the Beyoglu district to an open square filled with tables and chairs shaded by trees. People are sitting outside in the sunshine, drinking Turkish coffee and eating pastries.

The main hub is in the nineteenth-century Palazzo Corpi, which used to be an old U.S. embassy and is incredibly grand - probably the grandest Soho House in the world, with lofty high ceilings and ornate, impressive rooms. It feels like you're stepping back in time when you enter.

The most stunning spot is actually right at the top: the rooftop bar and restaurant, Mandolin. While all the bedrooms are stocked with shakers and mixers for whipping up cocktails, there's nothing like sipping my favourite Picante de la Casa - a chili margarita made with a twist - with the magnificent city views as a backdrop. The late summer afternoon's heat is gently cooled by the subtle breeze rising from the Bosphorus. Look out over the Istanbul skyline silhouetted with mosques, towers and bridges dating back many hundreds of years. As the sun sets, it all has an air of eastern promise and romanticism that's utterly unforgettable.

"It's probably the grandest Soho House in the world, with lofty high ceilings and ornate, impressive rooms."

POPPY DELEVINGNE

HOTEL BEL-AIR

The flight is coming in to land, Los Angeles is stretching out beneath me and I have butterflies. Is it the anticipation of the In-N-Out cheeseburger that I'm so desperately craving? Or is it the longing for that feeling of warm sunshine on my face, adding lashings of freckles to my already impressive collection? As the cab pulls up to the Hotel Bel-Air, I realise that, in fact, this is it: I'm coming home. If home were indeed candy-coated and sparkly and brimming with swans.

The first thing I do is order a freshly squeezed watermelon juice and take off into the gardens. Are you sure I'm not in Neverland? I stumble upon hidden alcoves and benches made for secret kisses beneath the purple bougainvillea.

Rooms are tucked among palm trees and exotic potted plants. At night, the whole place is sprinkled with fairy lights and romance. Everything buzzes and trickles, with creatures making their happy homes and fountains in abundance. I leap onto the bed deep in seventy-eight pillows, so crisp and so clean, while the most charming of bellboys lights the fire. Cosy just took on a whole new meaning.

I love finding places in LA that hold a little history. The pool house, surrounded by avocado trees, used to be the Bel-Air stables back in the 1920s. And one of the suites, the old Bel-Air sales offices, has its original beautiful wooden ceiling still intact in all its glory. Marilyn Monroe did her very last photo shoot here six weeks before she died. And I'm pretty sure Grace Kelly would have loved the suite they named after her, with hand-painted flowers all over the walls; the place is all about princesses.

The night draws in, and I head to the bar to drown myself in a bowl of red wine and another of truffle fries. Live jazz music is pouring into my ears, as iconic pictures by Norman Seeff, of Tina Turner and Ray Charles, look on by candlelight. This place is always overflowing with characters, stories and gossip.

I'm pretty sure I don't remember stumbling back to my delicious den, but suddenly morning is seeping in through my windows, and outside it's so still I feel like I'm on the top of the world. So tranquil, so calm. And all I want to do is melt into these powder-pink flamingo-coloured walls and disappear.

"As the cab pulls up to the Hotel Bel-Air, I realise that, in fact, this is it: I'm coming home. If home were indeed candy-coated and sparkly and brimming with swans."

ANYA HINDMARCH

HÔTEL LA MAMOUNIA

I love Marrakech. It's less than a four-hour flight from London, but when you step off the plane, it's a totally different climate, a place of palm trees and hot African sun, and it feels almost as if time has stood still. That's especially true at La Mamounia. It was the epicentre of that time in the 1970s when Morocco was such a jet-set location - the Marrakech of Yves Saint Laurent and the Rolling Stones. That glamour and exoticism that drew them here is still tangible; you can feel it in the walls of the hotel somehow.

I've been back to stay here many times, but I remember on my first visit being absolutely wowed by the location, tucked away in these enormous gardens, yet so close to the old medina. You get the best of both worlds: space, peace and garden views, whilst still having the bustling ancient city to explore just steps away.

My favourite room to stay in is one of the suites overlooking the gardens. They are big inside and out, and I always feel I could easily settle in for days. I like just sitting on the terrace, letting the sun soak into my bones as breakfast, wrapped in so much starched linen, and an endless stream of little treats - fresh oranges, Moroccan biscuits - appears. It's a real balm to the soul after a busy time. For the ultimate rejuvenation, having a *hammam* in the spa here is a bit like being reborn.

One of my favourite things to do, however, is to walk to the end of the gardens, past the olive trees and orange blossoms, and look back at the hotel while listening to the sounds of the world outside on the other side of the walls. There's nothing more evocative than the call to prayer reverberating from all sides of the city, slightly jarringly out of sync and out of tune. But for me it's the birds that make Marrakech. They are the sound of the city, and that, combined with the bright cobalt-blue skies and dry, restorative heat, never fails to make me happy.

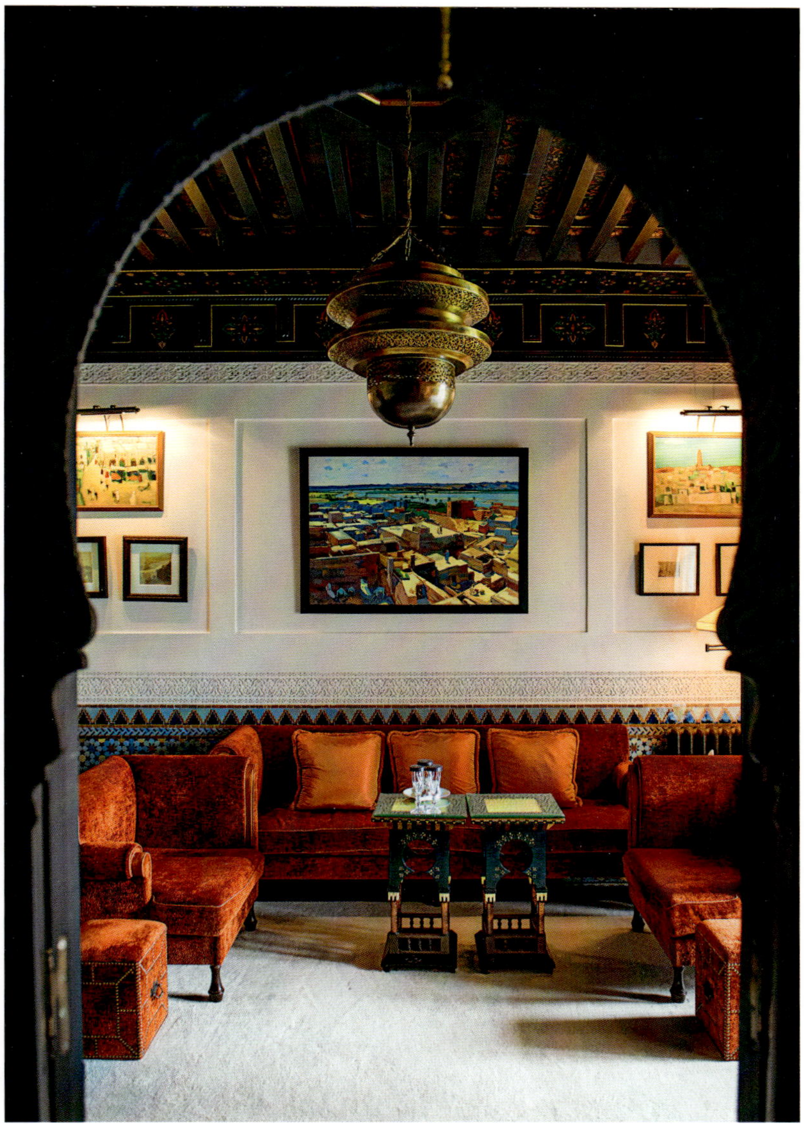

JAMES NORTON & JESSIE BUCKLEY

HAM YARD HOTEL

There's something special - and a little decadent - about checking into a hotel in your own city. Even strolling through Soho on our way to Ham Yard, along familiar streets that we regularly walk and cycle up and down, it all feels a bit different, like we are tourists rediscovering our home town. As everyone knows, London is an extraordinary and exciting place, but it's easy to forget that when you live here, easy to take this amazing city for granted.

Ham Yard itself is tucked into its own little square, and as you turn the corner here, it's hard to believe that this calm, quiet oasis - oak trees surrounded by shaded tables, a perfect place for a relaxed drink - exists so close to the hustle and bustle of Soho and Piccadilly Circus. And like Soho, the hotel constantly surprises at every turn: each piece of art, each room filled with individuality, with the kind of statement pieces you wish you could pull off in your own place but would never have the confidence to try. It feels grand and decadent without ever feeling alienating or pompous. In a way, Ham Yard epitomises London itself, mixing innovation, vitality and youth with tradition, heritage and class.

Yet although you're in the very heart of the city, it's all too tempting not to leave the hotel at all. And maybe that's the real beauty of staying in your home town: There's no pressure to race around exploring it. So instead, you properly relax and take a bubble bath in the enormous tub, have a perfect massage in the spa, eat breakfast on the balcony overlooking the rooftops, reading the Sunday papers in the sunshine, munching on the best eggs Benedict in town. And try all the cocktails at the bar - then try them all again!

AYER, HOY Y SIEMPRE...
SOLEDAD Y MUERTE

"Ham Yard epitomises London itself, mixing innovation, vitality and youth with tradition, heritage and class."

ACK
50 FT.
MAN

FLORENCE WELCH

CHATEAU MARMONT

I remember the first time I stayed at Chateau Marmont. It seemed like the haunted hotel ride at Disneyland and had an air of faded glamour about it - a sense of being lost and found at the same time. I remember singing at the piano one night, in the darkened living room, and I had the distinct impression that all the Chateau's hallways and passages led to rooms that were full of bright and brilliant yet chaotic people, all of whom had somehow converged at this one place on Sunset Boulevard: half sanctuary, half madhouse. I love staying in one of the big, beautiful blue rooms on the top floor, with their plush blue sofas and fires that I can never figure out how to turn on.

I was at the Chateau around the time of the Grammys one year, and we all went to one of the afterparties, an occasion that resulted in me lying face down in a bathtub - luckily it was empty. My other memory from that night is of Baz Luhrmann doing a spectacular Mick Jagger impression far too close to the balcony for my liking. Then a few days later, we managed to miss all the Oscars afterparties, and I ended up back in my room at the Chateau dressed like a superhero unicorn from a 1970s sci-fi series. Generally, I dress up in LA anyway. It's a city that changes your colour palette, and I feel I can dress more outrageously here. There was another occasion, a rather embarrassing moment, when I ended up doing squat thrusts in front of Josh Hartnett.

The garden is a great place to people-watch, to see which producer or actress or model or befuddled pop star (i.e., me) is sitting out there. I once even bumped into the guy who wrote 'You've Got the Love'. So my advice is to head here after you check in, jet-lagged and feeling pretty weird; it settles you nicely into LA. Then you should check out Musso & Frank's, on Hollywood Boulevard, which I love - the tuna salads are to die for! At the Chateau I usually order a plate of *arancini* and fresh lemonade. When we're being civilised, the band and I drink dirty martinis, though there have been nights when we've ordered oversized bottles of vodka at ungodly hours… Oh, how I'd like to thank and apologise to all those lovely members of staff who catered to us on those somewhat saturated mornings! As for sleep, well, if there has been a big party, I leave a little shaken, though shaken up in a good way.

“I remember the first time I stayed at Chateau Marmont. It seemed like the haunted hotel ride at Disneyland and had an air of faded glamour about it - a sense of being lost and found at the same time.”

Bar Marmont

ALICE TEMPERLEY

CHEVAL BLANC COURCHEVEL

Skiing from Cheval Blanc Courchevel is not like skiing from anywhere else. It is completely delicious, utterly spoiling. Each morning your very own ski butler lays everything out - skis, preheated boots, poles - all by a little flag with your room number on it. So after breakfast, off you go downstairs in fluffy slippers, and the butler slips on those toasty boots, and tucks in trousers, and clips up skis, and away you go, straight onto the slopes.

The hotel itself sits at the top of the town - the highest of the four Courchevels, Courchevel 1850 - behind mounds of snow, a huge disco ball-like mirrored horse standing proudly outside, surveying its storybook surroundings. Inside, there are roaring fires, smartly dressed guests and smiling staff everywhere. Everything here is done with unbelievable attention to detail - my martini at the bar is shaken with more skill than I've ever seen. Even the snow outside is well-groomed, perfectly manicured and blindingly white.

But what else would you expect from the people behind the likes of Louis Vuitton and Moët Hennessy? The look, naturally, is supremely tasteful: a modern take on the traditional chalet with lots of fine art and sculptures, beautiful furniture and fur throws. The spa is huge, and massages take place lying on one fluffy duvet with another on top - it's like being hugged by a cloud.

The two Michelin-starred restaurant Le 1947 is incredible and looks almost like something out of *Star Wars*, with tables set on beautiful white stone circles, mirrored by the big circular lamps hanging above. Braised chicory quince juice soup with gold leaf floating on top is followed by smoked chard with bone marrow mousse and caviar grains, truffled gnocchi with melted leeks and Jerusalem artichoke. It really is the most luxurious thing ever.

But if you only order one dish, make it the profiteroles covered in hot chocolate. They are the best profiteroles I've ever had in my life - and for all the truffles and caviar, the most delicious thing here. And that's saying something.

JEREMY IRONS

PALÁCIO BELMONTE

With my job, I stay in some of the most glorious places in the world, but Palácio Belmonte was like nothing I had ever encountered before. I was in the Portuguese capital making *Night Train to Lisbon*, and as soon as I saw this historic noble palace, built in 1449, I wanted to stay here. It feels like a private house with a slightly chaotic but hugely welcoming atmosphere, and each of the eleven suites is different. My favourite - the Bartolomeu de Gusmão suite - is spread over three floors in a seventh-century Moorish tower with tiled floors, big shutters and simple period furniture. One more flight up the circular stone staircase leads to a roof terrace, from where I can survey the old port and peer into surrounding courtyards. If the weather is warm, I could sling a hammock and sleep there.

I'd spent time in Lisbon filming *The House of the Spirits* some years before but had never discovered Old Lisbon. Staying at the Belmonte, I started a love affair with this part of the city, which has not been spoilt by over-restoration and still has the spirit of the nineteenth century. I enjoy watching trams nudge their way through impossibly narrow streets and wandering to the weekend market just five minutes away. I enjoy exploring the surrounding streets and spying on people living as they have for hundreds of years. I enjoy poking around in local antiques shops and eating in nearby restaurants. But most of all, I enjoy sitting crammed into a neighbourhood bar, listening to some of the greatest fado singing and having that wonderful sound open up to me like never before.

Within the Palácio itself, I have so many favourite spots, depending on the light and the time of day: breakfasting on the terrace, sitting reading in one of the little nooks - the library has more than four thousand books - or sipping Champagne by one of the fires, talking with the owners, Frederic Coustols and his wife, Maria Mendonca, about their extraordinary lives.

Ultimately, this is a hotel where you live rather than just stay. And living at the Palácio Belmonte is like living in the middle of a favourite book you are reading. You escape into it and never want it to end.

EVA LONGORIA

ONE&ONLY PALMILLA

I'm a Texan girl, from a Mexican-American family, living in LA - so Los Cabos is one of my all-time favourite places to go. I visit at least twice a year. It's such an easy hop for Angelenos and Texans, but most of all, Mexico has the best beaches in the whole world - I'm not biased, I promise - and here is no exception.

A vacation is not a vacation without a beach, but beyond the honeyed, sugar-like sand, One&Only Palmilla is breathtaking, the service incomparable, the food amazing and the weather perfect - the sun is always shining in Cabo.

I've been coming to the hotel for so long that it feels like my second home, and every time I'm here I feel very happy. My main goal when I arrive is to relax, so I try to spend as much time as humanly possible in the spa. Even if you're not having one of the treatments that use local herbs and even chocolate oil, it's worth walking into, because it's so beautiful: private villas for treatments, set in palm-shaded courtyards, massage beds beneath thatched cabanas, and the whole place smells *amazing*.

When I'm not in the spa, I'm outside: on my balcony, in the pool, at the beach, eating in the shade of a beachside cantina, then slipping straight back into the sunshine.

Mexico has so many magical places - for culture, for food, for music - but for me this is Mexico at its most special. It's a country that gives me a big hug every time I'm here.

BRYAN FERRY

MANDARIN ORIENTAL BANGKOK

When I think of the Mandarin Oriental in Bangkok, the Frank Sinatra album *Songs for Swingin' Lovers!* comes to mind - romantic, sophisticated, nostalgic, but with a certain lightness of touch too.

I first stayed here in the mid-1970s, when I was on tour in the Far East. I'd heard many great things about this fabulous hotel in Bangkok - the best in the world, they'd said - and I was curious to see if it lived up to its reputation. From the moment I arrived at the Oriental, I felt I was in a very special place. To start, the location is fabulous: looking out over the slowly winding Chao Phraya River, busy with boats of every shape and size. It's a fascinating scene, and there's nothing better than sitting on the terrace with a cool drink, gazing at life going by on the water.

Floating across the river in the hotel's classic little teak boat to the spa, set in a group of old-fashioned Thai houses on the opposite bank, is an experience too, and I always feel a great sense of well-being just arriving there. The spa itself is terrific and has every type of massage known to man - Swedish, Ayurvedic, Balinese, Hawaiian Lomilomi and, of course, Thai - although I find that one of the best ways to get rid of jet lag is actually to hit the tennis courts next door.

Architecturally, the Oriental represents the best of both worlds: modern and traditional. I've stayed in both parts, and it's hard to say which I prefer. The suites in the modern River Wing have amazing views of the Chao Phraya, and their cool restraint is in wonderful contrast to the intricate colonial charm of those in the Authors' Wing. The airy, white-rattan furniture-filled lounge still resonates with the glamour of Noël Coward and W. Somerset Maugham, just two of the many writers who have found inspiration here. One of my favourite spots in the hotel, however, is the more moody Bamboo Bar, where they make an excellent martini, and where you can live out the perfect *Man with the Golden Gun* 007 moment.

ORIENTAL

BETH DITTO

ACE HOTEL PORTLAND

I moved to Portland in 2003, back when I thought of it as a big little city. It's a bigger little city now, and getting bigger and bigger. In my time here, it's gone from being this under-the-radar place in Oregon to being the byword for hipsterdom. The TV series *Portlandia*, which satirises the city, is funny because it's so true! But all the reasons why it's funny are why it's amazing to live here. It's an incredible place if you're vegetarian or vegan, for activism and body positivity, to be queer - it's a mecca for any kind of alternative lifestyle.

My home is in North Portland and I often hang out here in an area they've now christened Alberta Arts District. It's so crazy when you're like, 'It's an arts district all of a sudden?' But there are so many funky neighbourhoods and different pockets in Portland, each with its own buzzing street.

Ace opened their second hotel in downtown Portland back in 2007 - the original is farther up the West Coast, in Seattle - and it's still a perennially cool place to be: There's a fresh, young vibe to it. Even though there are now Ace hotels all over - I especially love the one in London - each one has a very Pacific Northwest attitude. And they'll always cut a deal for a band to stay, which is really cool.

The music scene is really alive in Portland. There are a million cool places to see bands - the Crystal Ballroom, in an old 1914 dance hall, is an institution. There's also brilliant record shopping and so many little DJ nights, since DJs are now the new bands. But the real reason Portland is such a beautiful, sweet place to me? It's home.

goodtimes
SUPPLY
ACE HOTEL PORTLAND

THEY SHOULD HAVE SERVED THAT CUP OF COFFEE
DICK CLUSTER
A
ENGINEERING ELECTRICITY-HUDSON

DAYTON OHIO
SEATTLE
JACKSONVILLE FLA.
MAY

HO

"Ace Hotel Portland is still
a perennially cool place to be:
There's a fresh, young vibe to it."

BAR

MUSIC
21 DESSA
23 LOVE GIGANTIC
24 DAVID JACOBS-STRAIN
25 STEELHEAD
26 KOBO TOWN
27 WILLIAM TYLER
SOFT METALS

PIZZA SALAD BEER WINE
KON TIKI 150 710
STORIES WE TELL 140 415 640
FAST AND FURIOUS 6 400 940
MUD 345 925
EPIC SAT SUN 120

PISTACHIOS
EARTH₂O

DAVID NICHOLLS

AMAN VENICE

I've visited Venice many times and used to associate its hotels with gloomy, tiny rooms, erratic plumbing and those waxy pastries for breakfast. The Aman isn't like that, not at all.

When you arrive by water taxi, bouncing across the lagoon as the light fades on a crisp, clear winter's afternoon, then creeping through the narrow canals of Cannaregio until the Grand Canal opens up before you, it soon becomes clear that this is something quite special. The hotel lies just beyond the Rialto Bridge, housed in the sixteenth-century Palazzo Papadopoli, where boats dock at a private pier that leads directly into the impossibly elegant, high-ceilinged entrance hall.

It's the kind of hotel that presents a dilemma: You never want to leave, yet there's so much to see. One hundred yards to the east is the great wide expanse of Campo San Polo and the Titians in the Frari. A short walk to the north there's the lovely, barely visited Campo San Giacomo dall'Orio. Heading west, you can wander around the market and eat wonderful *cicchetti* in the celebrated All'Arco: *baccalà*, fresh prawns with garlic and parsley, and rich, salty anchovies.

After a breakfast of fresh fruit and flaky pastries in the beautiful Piano Nobile Lounge that overlooks the canal, we head off to see the Carpaccios at the Accademia, then drink the fantastic coffee at Caffè Rosso on Campo Santa Margherita, a little off the tourist track - the kind of place where you can, for a moment, imagine that you actually live here.

Unlike so many other grand hotels, there's never the sensation that you've been locked overnight in a museum. The surroundings are undeniably spectacular - gilded ceilings and brilliant chandeliers, sweeping staircases, that gorgeous dining room and rooftop terrace - but it's stylish without being chilly or pretentious, traditional without feeling stuffy or out of date.

On the last morning, keen to make the most of our time, we rise early and take a long, long walk to the city's easternmost tip, the church of San Pietro di Castello and its crumbling cloister, a place that has that combination of beauty and melancholy particular to Venice. Then we take a slow, meandering stroll home, getting lost on purpose on the way.

“When you arrive by water taxi, bouncing across the lagoon as the light fades on a crisp, clear winter's afternoon, it soon becomes clear that this is something quite special.”

KATE MOSS

AMILLA FUSHI

I love the Maldives - the beauty, the peacefulness, the wildlife, the privacy - but mostly the water; the water here is like nowhere else in the world. It's an overused phrase in these islands, but Amilla Fushi really is paradise: the most idyllic and relaxing place in the world. Some people worry that there's nothing to do in the Maldives, but I never have a dull moment at Amilla Fushi: snorkelling with turtles and sharks, fishing, a boat trip at sunset - all sorts of water sports. Under, over and on that astonishing water, there's so much to do.

Of course, when it comes to eating, the fish here is incredible too. I have sushi at Wok almost every day: Maldivian spicy yellowfin tuna sashimi, local reef fish tempura. But there are lots of lovely places to choose from, including a brilliant restaurant from Australian chef Luke Mangan. I love the variety.

Amilla Fushi was co-founded by innovative hotelier Tom McLoughlin, and he's everything that makes his hotels great: generous, with great taste and amazing ideas. There's none of the usual thatched villas and Robinson Crusoe castaway vibe here; instead there are sharp, modern houses as white as the sand on the beaches.

Our smiley butler Saddam is so fabulous, I always want to pack him up in my suitcase and take him home. Or even better, just stay here forever, drinking piña coladas on the beach and looking out across the infinite blue water from the deck of our home on stilts. That's the dream.

LAURA BAILEY

THE GREENWICH HOTEL

I nearly didn't make it to New York. Five cancelled flights, as snowboarders cruised down a silenced Fifth Avenue. Whiteout. Waiting for my luck to change, I hadn't dared admit to myself how much I missed Manhattan.

No waiting lover or friendly reunion, just the smiles of strangers and the flutter of adventure as I checked in to my single girl's room at The Greenwich, created by Robert de Niro in artsy downtown Tribeca back in 2008. Plans snow-cancelled, I slunk sulkily into shiny new winter boots to trudge past the Jurassic snorting snowploughs in moonlight live-action, spying on ever-glamorous New York couples vainly slip-sliding in search of cabs as the fairy-lit bars faded to black. I circled back to Locanda Verde, the restaurant at The Greenwich, in ecstatic nostalgia for my NYC twenties, when I accidentally-on-purpose missed a plane home and simply stayed, on a wish and a prayer, piecing together the jigsaw puzzle of my own American dream. In those days, Tribeca was all grown-up - the neighbourhood JFK Jr. and Carolyn Bessette prowled possessively in weekend khaki and corduroy en route to breakfast at Bubby's or cocktails at Odeon - and where I dreamt of a *loft*, a concept so seductive to an English runaway with bohemian pretensions.

The Greenwich taps into the rich, artistic cinephile personality of the neighbourhood and is the not-so-well-kept secret hideaway of fashion and film industry insiders drawn to its old-school discreet charm and unpretentious homey style - a rose-tinted living room and blue velvet nooks, and a somewhat mythical wabi-sabi penthouse presiding over the streets below. Here I find my early-morning and late-night corner beside the fire, the empathetic waiter who knows my breakfast double espresso coffee confessional, and who pours tequila on the rocks in the witching hours without asking.

Back home in London, I don't want to talk about New York. I just want to go back to The Greenwich and steal a secret day or two when no one knows I'm there. No past lives or pictures or godchildren - just messing around in a city that was once my home, where every room is a room with a view and where some kind of wonderful hotel can make it feel like the first time - again.

ELIE SAAB

FOUR SEASONS HOTEL GEORGE V

I first came to Paris from Beirut when I was seventeen to go to design school. I have very good memories of that initial taste of the City of Light and knew immediately that I'd come back. After all, it is the fashion capital of the world. Since that moment, my dream was to establish my brand and although I returned to Lebanon to launch my label the following year, French women, with their carefree attitudes and simplicity, have always been central to my designs.

I started staying at the Hotel George V in 2000 when I began showing my collections during Paris Haute Couture Fashion Week. It's one of my favourite hotels in the world. I love its elegant white stone Art Deco architecture, its gilded interiors, and its remarkable art collection - not to mention its wonderful location in the heart of Paris's Golden Triangle, in the middle of the Champs-Élysées, Avenue Montaigne and Avenue George V. I love the eighth arrondissement so much, in fact, that I've since bought an apartment nearby, and in 2015 opened my second Paris boutique right next door to the hotel.

I still adore the George V - it's like a second home to me. I can spend hours with family and friends talking and relaxing in Le Bar. Or else I simply slip in to see the exquisite flowers created by the hotel's artistic director, Jeff Leatham. The whole scheme changes every three weeks, and there are hundreds of vases in just the lobby alone. It truly is spectacular, and on each occasion, no matter how many times I've visited, it never fails to wow me, just like the whole of the George V itself.

ROSAMUND PIKE

AMAN SUMMER PALACE BEIJING

This place is a glorious, surprising hymn to everything that is beautiful and mysterious about China.

Leaving behind the thrilling dusty hit of Beijing proper, the first thing that always strikes me about this hotel is the delicate smell of incense and perfumed oils that makes you want to drink the air.

It is built around courtyards, which, according to Chinese design, give a sense of balance to those living within them. While being driven by rickshaw and carriage to your room, the eye wanders over carved wooden architecture, a subtle interplay of reds and blues, a miniature lake with overhanging willows and people enjoying incredibly beautiful tea.

There's a little bit of adventure and mystery about everything here: the mind-boggling gorgeousness of the Imperial Suite, where the simplicity and flow of its many rooms make it seem like it goes on forever; dinners in secret rooms or under the stars that feel like pieces of theatre in which you are part of the production; dishes that overwhelm in their deliciousness, beautifully presented and excitingly unfamiliar; the sensational art of Chinese dry massage, where your body is expertly rearticulated through dark blue silk pyjamas.

The hotel discreetly offers privileged access to the gardens of the Summer Palace next door. At dawn the only souls joining you on the banks of Kunming Lake to take in the pleasure gardens built for Empress Dowager Cixi are local joggers and fearless year-round swimmers. At the end of the day, you can return to breathe in the scent of peonies in full riotous bloom, and watch the sun setting over the marble boat before knocking on a wall to escape through a hidden door back into the sanctuary of the hotel.

On the last night, a delicate miniature padlock - possibly reminiscent of a Qing Dynasty safety pin - is left on the pillow in my beautiful vaulted bedroom. Perhaps it's asking me to keep some of the Aman Summer Palace's secrets. I will. But I can say that they are worth unlocking for yourself. This is a place of enchantment like no other.

“At dawn the only souls joining you on the banks of Kunming Lake to take in the pleasure gardens are local joggers and fearless year-round swimmers.”

有長可取不虛生

MICHAEL MORPURGO

GRAND HOTEL A VILLA FELTRINELLI

I wonder if there can be anywhere more gracious, more palatial, more cosseting than Villa Feltrinelli on Lake Garda. I had just finished a book - my excuse for staying the weekend in such sumptuous surroundings. I deserved it, I told myself. Further, I had another book in my mind that I wanted to work up, and I needed peace and tranquillity to dream myself into it.

Happily, this hotel has wonderful literary credentials too. It was the home of Signor Feltrinelli, the great Italian publisher who had printed Pasternak's *Doctor Zhivago* and Lampedusa's *The Leopard*. Winston Churchill - who wrote a fair bit too, among other things - had come to stay to paint pictures of Lake Garda. D. H. Lawrence lived nearby for a while, where he apparently penned *Women in Love*. And thereby hangs an interesting coincidence: My wife, Clare, happens to be the daughter of Sir Allen Lane, founder of Penguin Books, who famously published D. H. Lawrence's *Lady Chatterley's Lover* and all his other novels too. So it boded well for us both.

I wish I could say ideas for the new book flowed easily. They flowed not at all. Rather, the wine flowed at our candlelit dinner table, the water lapping lazily, the sun going down over the lake. It was one of the greatest feasts we had ever had - the asparagus unforgettable - and the best Tignanello I ever drank. Then to bed, where, lulled by a gently sighing breeze in the trees, sleep came easily.

The next morning after breakfast I had my notebook out, but the sun and the pool beckoned. So we swam and talked and read and sipped lemonade with apple juice and grenadine. After lunch we set off on a boat, returning in time for a Bellini or two and another wonderful dinner. My notebook remained empty. How could I write in such a place where you have to live every moment only for the moment?

Our stay inspired me in other ways. It lifted the spirits, 'summoned up the blood'. Once home, I wrote with a will and filled my notebook. All right, so it may not have been *Women in Love* - rather, my own retelling of *Pinocchio*. I'm telling you, Pinocchio, who had sybaritic tendencies rather like me, would have loved the Villa Feltrinelli.

La Contessa

ANNIE CLARK

HOTEL SAINT CECILIA

Austin was like Oz to us kids growing up in Dallas: mythic. I ended up writing my record *St. Vincent* there in the spring of 2013 and became friends with hotelier Liz Lambert. Liz embodies everything that is so authentic and big-hearted about Texas. She's the campfire around which so many musicians, artists, cowboys and characters circle.

One of her hotels in town, the Saint Cecilia, is an homage to rock-and-roll decadence. Named after the patron saint of music and poetry, and inspired by the Rolling Stones' time at Villa Nellcôte on the Côte d'Azur recording *Exile on Main St*, it's a place where debauchery and beautiful china can coexist.

Every detail inside the rooms is elegant but approachable, from the kimono robes in the shower to the crisp linens and the bath products. Downstairs there's a huge library of vinyl for guests to peruse. I once spent a night lying on the floor of my room with Nina Simone playing on repeat on my turntable.

The hotel is tucked away on a residential street just off South Congress. You can walk by on the sidewalk and look into its stately open-air courtyard with French bistro tables. This is the place where people love to congregate and have a laugh. Another city or setting might invite pomp and pretense from the patrons; not so at 'the Saint'. Everyone operates on the 'a friend of Liz is a friend of mine' principle. On given nights, I've been sat near Robert Plant while he regaled us with stories of the Zeppelin days; or with Jill Abramson and the late, great David Carr and his wife, Jill, talking world politics; or with my oldest friends just reminiscing. It's quiet and magical - and sometimes loud and magical, if the right crew is around laughing and drinking and smoking until the early hours of the morning.

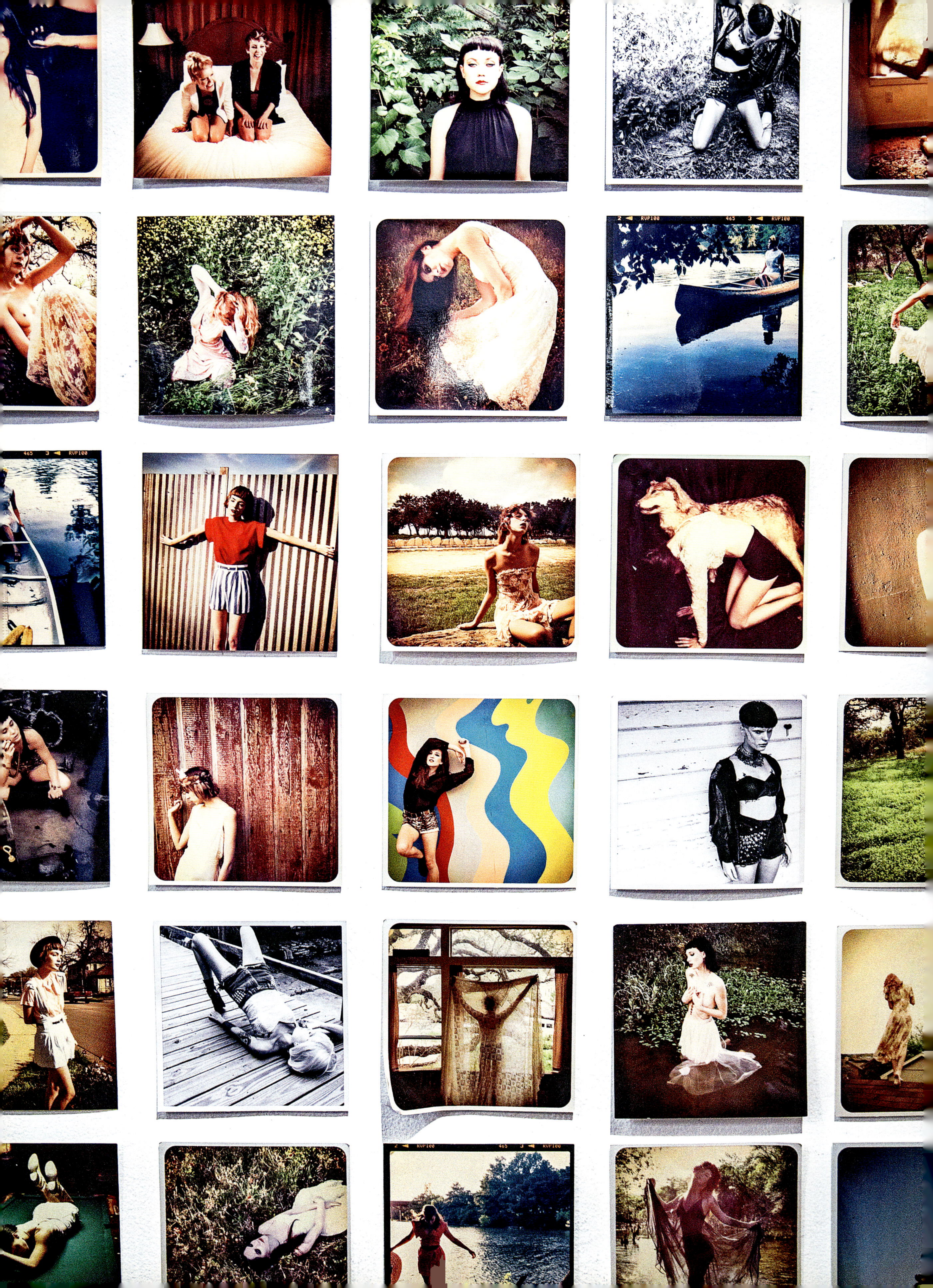

SOUL

SANTAL 33
SANTAL 33
SANTAL 33

PATRICK FRENCH

SUJÁN RAJMAHAL PALACE

There is nothing understated about Suján Rajmahal Palace. It is an extravaganza conjured out of Rajasthan's royal history, more of a reinvention than a nostalgic recreation. From the moment you arrive, you feel as if you are in a modern version of the past.

I first visited when it was on the verge of opening and was impressed by the way the hotel succeeded in being sumptuous while retaining a feeling of being at home. Conceived in the eighteenth century as a princely retreat, it has suites named after more recent glamorous guests such as Jackie Kennedy and Lord Mountbatten, and even today you are as likely to bump into a member of the Jaipur royal family as a visitor from abroad.

Rajmahal feels sensory as well as palatial: Each part of the building produces an aesthetic impact, an incandescence softened by refracted light. It has as many colours as Holi. In the breakfast room, Diana Vreeland's famed injunction, 'pink is the navy blue of India', has been taken to heart: It is called 51 Shades of Pink, a visual explosion veering from fuchsia to magenta, befitting the roseate city of Jaipur.

A day out in the swirl and dust can be a little too much, and Rajmahal Palace is the ideal antidote. Like all of the Suján properties, it has spirited old-school staff, twirled moustaches at the ready, who practise an informal perfection - a kind of service that is one step up from formal perfection. I see a gimlet appearing in the Polo Bar, a stately figure floating over a black-and-white checkerboard marble floor, a succulent dish of *jungli maas* served out in the colonnade of airy blue.

JAIPUR
1

STELLA TENNANT

LISMORE CASTLE

An invitation to Lismore Castle should never be turned down - and when the crenellated castle is not rented out for others to make their own, it's the Irish home of my cousin William Burlington, son of the twelfth Duke of Devonshire, and his wife, Laura. When we stay, children always massively outnumber parents, but all are absorbed into the endless turrets and wings.

We arrive to fires blazing and tea waiting. It's not just any tea but a significant event, consisting of sandwiches, cakes and fresh scones with cream, all served in the drawing room by the bay window. The vertiginous views down to the aptly named Blackwater soften into the skyline of the Knockmealdown Mountains. In the middle ground is an outrageous pink cloud of a magnolia tree planted by my late grandmother, Deborah Devonshire.

This ancient place, of which the oldest part was built by Prince John in 1185, sits high above the River Blackwater in County Waterford. It's a strategic situation, giving it views up and down the river where marauding Danes once roamed. The castle is steeped in stories. It has been home to bishops, tobacco smokers (Sir Walter Raleigh), scientists (Robert Boyle), prime ministers (William Cavendish), dancers (Fred Astaire's sister Adele married the younger son of the ninth Duke) and plain old aristocrats.

Today, you can peel back the layers of history from the deep comfort of the sofa by the fire, surrounded by seventeenth-century Flemish tapestries of scenes from *Don Quixote*, or as you lie in a steaming bath, with photographs of Adele and Fred Astaire dancing around you.

William's addition of the gallery, Lismore Castle Arts, gives it yet another layer; the exhibitions of international contemporary artists bring visitors from near and far. The gallery leads directly into the walled garden, which is my idea of horticultural perfection, combining a perfect kitchen plot with extravagant border planting. Bathed in the Gulf Stream, palms and other exotic plants flourish, and the magnificent camellias and magnolias make an idyllic backdrop for Easter egg hunts.

If this were commune living, I'd sign up today. But in reality, it is expertly run by Denis, the mystical figure behind the castle's inner workings, and his brilliant team. Luxury and culture make the perfect bedfellows in this fascinating place.

County Waterford, Ireland *lismorecastle.com*

JUMBLE CAT

FELLINI
MADE IN ITALY

CARA DELEVINGNE

PARROT CAY

As soon as the boat pulls up to the pier, I jump out, plant my feet in the sand and sprint into the bluest sea. It's the sheer sense of calm, the peace, that sets this apart from other islands in the Caribbean - being able to run along the beach to the beat of Pharrell on my headphones and not see anyone for miles, just run and run with nothing but wildlife and the lush island greenness that goes right down to the water.

That's not to say there isn't a lot to do. We windsurf, we play tennis, we walk around the island and kayak down the river running through it. We go deep-sea fishing, and I reel in a huge fish - a barracuda! There's plenty of fish on the menu too, whether fresh from the barbecue at Lotus, my favourite restaurant by the pool, or the wicked fish and chips from room service, pure hole-up-in-your-villa comfort food. And you couldn't find a more picturesque place to hole up, dressed all in white. It's just ten steps from your room to the beach, where there are two sun loungers waiting under an umbrella. But it's well worth leaving to walk up the hill to the incredible spa. I go every day for a different treatment - the reflexology is really good, but the COMO Shambhala Bath begins with a scrub and a soak that makes me the softest I've ever been in my life. It ends with a soul-soothing full-body massage - and after each one they serve the most amazing ginger tea.

But if you only do one thing, lie on the beach all day, from sunrise to sunset, because it's the most beautiful beach in the world. Don't even think of moving. Just stay right there and watch the stars come out at night, every one of them blazing across the sky so brightly, like nothing else in the world.

"If you only do one thing at Parrot Cay, lie on the beach all day, from sunrise to sunset. Don't even think of moving. Just stay right there and watch the stars come out at night."

SIR PAUL SMITH

CLARIDGE'S

It's an overused word these days, but Claridge's truly is iconic. Even before visiting for the first time, I'd heard so much about its fascinating history that as soon as I stepped into the polished revolving doors, I knew I was entering somewhere very special.

I first stayed about twenty years ago but had been going for drinks or dinner for some time before then. I'm not a big drinker, but tea in the Reading Room is a great treat for anyone visiting London.

I've been so many times since my first stay that I've lost count. My wife, Pauline, and I have been together since I was twenty-one, but we still like to go on dates. Claridge's is somewhere we love to visit, particularly if we're celebrating.

I love the Art Deco feel that runs through the hotel. From the black-and-white tiled foyer to the mirrored ballroom where I've held fashion shows, everything about it is reminiscent of that stylish period. The history attached to the whole place also comes through in the countless interesting people who have stayed over the years: from film stars such as Cary Grant, Richard Burton and Elizabeth Taylor to politicians like Winston Churchill, who moved in after the war - and so many more.

Even now, every visit feels like a treat. When service elsewhere has become very rehearsed, formulaic and homogenised, Claridge's has so much personality - especially John, who works in the lift. Many of the staff have been here for such a long time that they are as much a part of the hotel's story as its famous guests. But ultimately, Claridge's is part of London's own story in a way that few others can claim to be.

CLARIDGE'S

the Fumoir

HUGH BONNEVILLE

SIX SENSES ZIGHY BAY

After a two-hour drive across the desert from Dubai, the road rises through the craggy peaks of the Al Hajar Mountains, until suddenly, cresting the summit, Zighy Bay opens up 300 metres below. And we stop, because it's here that our paraglider pilot, Itso, clips me onto his wings to swoop and soar and float down to the beach far below. It's certainly a different and special way to arrive at a hotel.

At sea level, stone villas cluster around a maze of sandy paths shaded by date palms like a traditional Omani fishing village, complete with wandering goats. Houses are rustic but a little more luxurious than your average fisherman's: chunky wooden furniture bound with rope, plunge pools and plenty of perfectly plumped burnt-orange cushions. And my son loves it. He buzzes from activity to activity: origami, feeding the goats, simple Arabic lessons, snorkelling trips and jungle gyms. My wife and I let our butler, Abilash, arrange everything, from a microlight flight to browse the hotel and the small town of Dibba to a sunset boat ride with chatty local fisherman Humaid.

Whatever, wherever, whenever we eat, the food is superb. We sit cross-legged at low beachside tables in Shua Shack for lamb that's been marinated in spices, wrapped in a banana leaf and cooked in a pit for seven hours. We feast on sensational shish kebabs and date crème brûlée at Spice Market. We drink in the view with our Basirina at Sense on the Edge, a mountaintop eyrie where the food is as spectacular as the panorama.

Back down to earth, and the spa is a lemongrass-scented haven to slow even the most stressed-out pulse. I zone out so completely during the Balinese massage that I only hope the therapist took my snoring as a compliment.

Radish

OLIVIA PALERMO

LE ROYAL MONCEAU

I stay at the Royal Monceau about four times a year - it really is my Paris home. It's quite different from your classic grand palace hotel in the French capital. Instead, it's modern, it's hip, and there's lots of style and personality in Philippe Starck's design. When I'm travelling, I think it's important to try all sorts of hotels - some bigger, some more boutique - but the Royal Monceau has that Goldilocks trick of being just right. Plus, the staff are really fantastic and friendly, and their warm welcome is so special to come back to - you appreciate that when you spend more nights in hotels than in your own bed, like I do.

I love trying a different room every time. There are also three incredible apartments, the Presidential Suites, each with its own look and feel. There might be a huge, prettily tufted pink headboard behind the bed, or a sleek mirrored dining table, and everywhere, buttery leathers, soft velvets and gleaming marble. But it's the little touches - the Evian and berries waiting for me, the TV in the bathroom so I can watch my favourite show, the Wi-Fi that with one click I'm in - that really make the Royal Monceau a home-from-home.

So much so that I tend to order room service - the saffron risotto is what I dream about when I'm not there. But the chef, Roberto Rispoli, is amazing, and his restaurant deservedly has a Michelin star. Downstairs, too, there's a brilliant gallery, the Art District, which showcases young artists, and one of the most beautiful stores in Paris: Le Royal Eclaireur. It has some incredible and under-the-radar designers - scarves from French illustrator Pierre-Louis Mascia, bags from VBH - as well as the likes of Peter Pilotto and Balmain.

From there, I love going for a stroll. The hotel is right by the Arc de Triomphe, and the Champs-Élysées is just two blocks away, but that's a bit like going to New York and heading to Times Square. Instead, I prefer to get lost in the charming side streets or wander over to the boutiques on Avenue Montaigne.

"I love trying a different room every time.
There might be a huge, prettily tufted
pink headboard behind the bed,
or a sleek mirrored dining table,
and everywhere buttery leathers,
soft velvets and gleaming marble."

TABITHA SIMMONS

1 HOTEL SOUTH BEACH

Miami does lobbies like nowhere else, and 1 Hotel South Beach is no exception. An expansive space of white and wood, with huge windows and big squishy sofas, it hums with conversation and beautiful people. But the thing I love most about it, which surprised me the first time I visited, is that it's actually all sustainable.

The reception desk is made from an old oak tree, and there's a wall that from a distance looks like artwork - a gigantic mural of a swimmer - but when you get closer you see that it's really moss. Off to one side is a juice bar to pick up that green cleanse on the way back from SoulCycle next door. Waiting outside is a fleet of Tesla electric cars to whizz silently around town.

It's green yet glamorous, fun but also fearsomely followed through: Room keys are fashioned out of recycled wood, and beds have hemp mattresses covered in organic linen. In the wardrobes are hangers cut from cardboard, made from old packaging, and in the shower there are sand timers set to five minutes. The bedrooms are huge and bright, airy and supremely calming - a refreshing change from Miami's usual high-tempo vibe.

Miami for me is always a beach fix, a blast of heat away from New York's winters. There's a string of hotels along this stretch of South Beach, and if you wander out from 1 Hotel, you're on the sand. But anyone can see Miami from sea level; the best view here is up on the roof - it's incredible. The whole of Miami stretches out below while I sit up here in the sky, sipping tequila and soda by the pool.

"The lobby of the 1 Hotel South Beach hums with conversation and beautiful people. But the thing I love most about it is that it's actually all sustainable."

SUPER
VACANT
3571
1028

SOPHIE DAHL

CLIVEDEN HOUSE

The story of Cliveden is a very English one, a tale of indomitable women, victims of circumstance and, at the beating heart of it, a building and garden of great Italianate loveliness, perched upon a bank of rolling green overlooking the Thames. The original house was built in 1666 by the Duke of Buckingham, but it was the American-born Nancy Langhorne who became its best-known châtelaine in 1906, when she married the second Viscount Astor, whose father had bought the property. She filled Cliveden with the sparky and erudite - Churchill, Roosevelt and Henry James - and made it so modern and comfortable that a posh English girl would have shrieked at the excess.

It was when Langhorne's son Bill was living here in 1961 that John Profumo, the Secretary of State for War, stumbled upon a topless teenage showgirl, Christine Keeler - a guest of Astor's osteopath who leased the estate's Spring Cottage. Their affair was to topple the British political establishment.

It's difficult not to think about all this history as you drive toward Cliveden. The air here is heady with an odd mixture of historic lust and something very U-rated. There is high opulence, but also games of hide-and-seek. The gardens can be packed with visitors, but there are also stolen moments to walk on shaded paths alone, imagining who went before.

Spring Cottage is a peach of a place, ripe for clandestine weekends or taming ducks on the riverbank with children. There is big comfort, but also a wonderful lack of preciousness. The kitchen shelves burst with thoughtful things (hot cross buns, macaroons, marshmallows), and you can call on people as you need. It's old-fashioned holidays, *Swallows and Amazons* style.

A recent massive and sensitive refurbishment has driven away the ghosts at Cliveden, and the main house is like a box of Turkish delight: winding cellars and rooms each with its own personality. There is something of the survivor about the place, something proud and gorgeous in that stone: gin fizz and Chaplin, Queen Victoria and, of course, those showgirls. If it can exist like a house party, tread that fine line of belonging to everybody and nobody, it will carry on regardless. It's a bit like an old beauty at a wedding whose stories you want to hear, and whose hand you want to hold.

THE MISTRESSES OF CLIVEDEN
THREE CENTURIES OF SCANDAL, POWER AND INTRIGUE
'Utterly fascinating and completely beguiling' Amanda Foreman
NATALIE LIVINGSTONE
NATALIE LIVINGSTONE

GUY RITCHIE

SONEVA FUSHI

Although Samuel Coleridge's *The Rime of the Ancient Mariner* and Yann Martel's *Life of Pi* offer a similar castaway adventure vibe, no fiction can really encapsulate the real-world wonder that is Soneva Fushi. Perhaps *The Swiss Family Robinson* or *Robinson Crusoe* come closer - but without the cannibalism and plus butlers! The most accurate analogy, however, is probably *Avatar*. When you arrive, it's like plugging into the Hometree; it's amazing how the human nervous system can connect with nature when you let it, and this is just the place for that. Rather than competing with nature's beauty, Soneva Fushi complements it. Here the beauty is bare: no harsh straight lines or modern angles. Instead, restaurants without walls invite organic gardens inside, and rough-hewn villas are built around elderly jungle trees, every structure unrefined and authentic.

My wife, Jacqui, and I first came to Soneva Fushi in December 2014, juggling three babies and way too may suitcases. Barefoot, we headed down the jetty, and our first impression was one of relief. The hotel is exactly what it purports to be: paradise. As soon as we set foot on the island, we always jump into the ocean, and the stress of the journey dissipates at first dunk. The mantra here is 'no shoes, no news' - and yes, once they come off, our shoes are relegated to the suitcase for the rest of the holiday. Villa number 14 on the sunrise side of the island is our favourite spot. The kids love the upstairs treehouse-inspired bedrooms under thatched roofs and swaying coconut palms.

Some of our most cherished moments at Soneva Fushi are our evening bike rides. We pack our pyjama-clad children into the trunks of our tricycles and ride the lily-lined paths to Bar(a) Bara, where they order chocolate cocktails (milkshakes) and we sit in hammocks over the dusky sapphire water and watch the sun melt into the horizon. And that's Soneva Fushi's secret: When you live slowly, you allow yourself the gift of time to appreciate everything to its fullest.

"Rather than competing with nature's beauty, Soneva Fushi complements it. Here the beauty is bare: no harsh straight lines or modern angles."

CONTRIBUTORS

WRITERS

ALESSANDRA AMBROSIO

UXUA Casa Hotel & Spa, Trancoso, Brazil

Born in Erechim, Brazil to parents of Italian and Polish descent, Alessandra Ambrosio emerged into the international modelling world as a part of the Brazilian invasion in the late 1990s. She has been a Victoria's Secret Angel for over ten years and lives in Los Angeles with her daughter, Anja. Her favourite country is Panama, where she says the loveliest spot is the secluded Contadora Beach.

LAURA BAILEY

The Greenwich, New York, United States

A model as well as a writer, Laura Bailey was born in London, where she now lives in Notting Hill. But, she says, 'New York has long had a hold on my heart. I arrived with an overnight bag for a shoot, aged twenty-three, and stayed for seven years. London, of course, is home, just as Paris will always be my runaway fantasy.'

HUGH BONNEVILLE

Six Senses Zighy Bay, Dibba Bayeh, Oman

As an understudy to Ralph Fiennes's Lysander, Hugh Bonneville began his stage career crashing a cymbal in *A Midsummer Night's Dream*. Now he is most often recognised as Lord Grantham in the hit TV series *Downton Abbey*. Hugh lives in West Sussex with his wife and son.

ANNIE CLARK

Hotel Saint Cecilia, Austin, United States

Musician and songwriter Annie Clark, a.k.a. St. Vincent, wrote the eponymous album that won her the Best Alternative Music Album award at the Grammys, as well as a nomination for Album of the Year by NME. Annie lives between Texas (where she hangs out in Austin whenever she can), LA and New York. Further afield, her favourite beach spot is Thailand.

SOFIA COPPOLA

Palazzo Margherita, Bernalda, Italy

Writer, producer and director Sofia Coppola grew up in Northern California. She studied fine art before writing and directing *The Virgin Suicides* and went on to win an Academy Award for *Lost in Translation*. Besides Italy, she loves 'the South of France, Belize and the Caribbean – the Turks and Caicos is so beautiful.'

SOPHIE DAHL

Cliveden House, Berkshire, United Kingdom

Model-turned-writer Sophie Dahl is a devoted home cook. She has written a number of recipe books and lives in the country with her husband, jazz musician Jamie Cullum, and their two daughters. When travelling overseas, she loves the Maldives: 'It's my idea of total paradise. I wobble everywhere barefoot on a bicycle with my babies in a basket on the back.'

CARA DELEVINGNE

Parrot Cay, Turks and Caicos Islands

One of the most recognisable faces in the world, Cara Delevingne has a burgeoning acting career in addition to her success as a model. She made her film debut in Joe Wright's *Anna Karenina* alongside Keira Knightley and recently won rave reviews as eighteen-year-old Margot in *Paper Towns*. Cara is also an accomplished singer and drummer.

POPPY DELEVINGNE

Hotel Bel-Air, Los Angeles, United States

Model, actress and designer Poppy Delevingne is a British Fashion Council Ambassador. When not in LA, she lives between London – 'I've spent two years renovating our house in Shepherd's Bush – now everything is candy-floss pink and covered in palm-tree print' – and the English countryside, 'which is all about bottomless bubble baths and cider.'

BETH DITTO

Ace Hotel Portland, United States

Singer-songwriter Beth Ditto is most notable for her work with the indie rock band Gossip. Now she's gone solo, but when not working, she holidays in Hawaii. 'I go to Oahu, but the whole country is lush. Avocados fall off trees as if it's no big deal, and there are flowers everywhere, geckos and chameleons – I mean, come on, it's out of control.'

LUKE EVANS

Soho House Istanbul, Turkey

Having started his career in London's West End, Welsh actor Luke Evans is best known for his role as the iconic dragon slayer and archery expert, Bard the Bowman, in the *Hobbit* trilogy. He received a Best Supporting Actor nomination at the British Independent Film Awards for his role in Ben Wheatley's suspense *High Rise*.

SEBASTIAN FAULKS

Ceylon Tea Trails, Hatton, Sri Lanka

Before quitting journalism to write full time, Sebastian Faulks was the first literary editor of *The Independent*. He is best known for his novels *Birdsong*, *Engleby* and *Human Traces* and was elected a Fellow of the Royal Society of Literature. When not writing, he likes to play tennis and cricket.

BRYAN FERRY

Mandarin Oriental Bangkok, Thailand

As the lead singer and songwriter in rock band Roxy Music, Bryan Ferry had three number-one albums and ten top 10 singles in the 1970s. These days, Bryan is based between London and Sussex. His all-time favourite holiday? 'I've been going to Mustique since 1973, but it's best in February, when most people have left and you can really relax.'

LIVIA FIRTH

Song Saa, Cambodia

A UN Leader of Change, Livia Firth is the founder of ethical brand consultancy Eco-Age. Her Green Carpet Challenge campaigns for ethical and sustainable fashion on the red carpet. As an Oxfam Global Ambassador, Livia has travelled to Ethiopia, Kenya, Bangladesh and Zambia. She lives in London with her husband, Colin, two children, one cat and four fish.

PATRICK FRENCH

Suján Rajmahal Palace, Jaipur, India

British writer and historian Patrick French is the author of a number of prize-winning books about Asia, including *India: A Portrait*. 'As a writer, I'm highly responsive to my physical surroundings when it comes to starting on the first page of a book. The ideal place for inspiration to write is probably rural England on a cool summer's day.'

ANYA HINDMARCH

Hôtel La Mamounia, Marrakech, Morocco

Designer Anya Hindmarch is known for her playful accessories which have a real sense of humour. As a passionate advocate of British design and the arts, she is also a UK trade ambassador, non-executive director of the British Fashion Council and trustee of both the Royal Academy of Arts and the Design Museum. Anya lives and works in London.

JEREMY IRONS

Palácio Belmonte, Lisbon, Portugal

British-born actor Jeremy Irons is renowned for his film, television and theatre performances. He won the Best Actor Academy Award for his performance as Claus von Bulow in *Reversal of Fortune*, and is a Golden Globe, Primetime Emmy and Tony Award winner. He is also the voice of Scar in Disney's *The Lion King*.

EVA LONGORIA

One&Only Palmilla, San José del Cabo, Mexico

A Golden Globe-nominated producer and director, Eva Longoria stars, produces and directs the hit comedy series *Telenovela*. The *Desperate Housewives* alum also directs the drama series *Devious Maids*. Through her charity, the Eva Longoria Foundation, she champions women, the Latino community and youth with special needs.

SIR ROGER MOORE

La Colombe d'Or, Saint-Paul-de-Vence, France

Best known for his work as James Bond, Roger Moore shot a total of seven films as the British secret agent. He was awarded a knighthood in 2003 for his charity work with UNICEF. Roger lives between Monaco and Crans-Montana, Switzerland, with his wife, Kristina, and is a proud grandfather of six.

ERDEM MORALIOGLU

Park Hyatt Tokyo, Japan

Fashion designer Erdem Moralioglu was born in Montreal to a Turkish father and English mother. His designs are best identified by their use of vibrant prints and experimental textiles. Where inspires him? 'The place that most moves me is Paris. I never understand how anyone can say it doesn't. It's the best city to explore and take in on foot.'

MICHAEL MORPURGO

Grand Hotel a Villa Fetrinelli, Lake Garda, Italy

The former Children's Laureate and bestselling author has written 130 books, including *War Horse*, which went on to become both a successful theatre production and feature film. He feels most inspired to write in the Camargue in the Languedoc region of southern France. 'I've just been working on a new story set there, inspired by the wonderful flamingos.'

KATE MOSS

Amilla Fushi, Maldives

One of the most iconic figures of the fashion industry, Kate Moss was born in Croydon, south-east London. Spotted at the age of fourteen, she set out on a modelling career which has seen her appear on over three hundred magazine covers as well as working with fashion houses including Calvin Klein, Chanel and Gucci.

DAVID NICHOLLS

Aman Venice, Italy

Author David Nicholls's novel *Us* was nominated for the Man Booker Prize, and both *One Day* and *Starter for Ten* have been adapted for film. David lives and works in north London, loves Paris in August and entertains fantasies about moving to Berlin. 'I love walking too – the Northumberland coast, the Dales and Lakes.'

BILL NIGHY

The Carlyle, New York, United States

Best known for his performance as aging rockstar Billy Mack in Richard Curtis's *Love Actually*, Bill Nighy has also appeared onscreen in *The Constant Gardner*, *The Best Exotic Marigold Hotel* and the Harry Potter series. His favourite place to relax is Paris: 'I love the width of the avenues and the cafés! I like cafés as much as I like anything else in the world. And obviously, Paris is the capital city of cafés.'

JAMES NORTON & JESSIE BUCKLEY

Ham Yard Hotel, London, United Kingdom

Yorkshire-raised James Norton and Irish-born Jessie Buckley played alongside each other in the critically acclaimed BBC mini-series *War and Peace*. James read theology at Cambridge before enrolling at the Royal Academy of Dramatic Art in London; his film credits include Mr Turner and Belle, while Jessie, also a RADA graduate, appeared on stage in Kenneth Branagh's *The Winter's Tale*.

OLIVIA PALERMO

Le Royal Monceau, Paris, France

Native New Yorker Olivia Palermo has gained international recognition as one of the fashion world's premier insiders. She has a jewellery collection with BaubleBar and her own fashion line with Nordstrom. Known for her style credentials, Olivia loves Japan for the unique variety of shops.

ROSAMUND PIKE

Aman Summer Palace Bejing, China

Having started her career on stage, Rosamund Pike received rave reviews as Helen in *An Education* alongside Carey Mulligan. She went on to star as Amy Dunne in box-office hit *Gone Girl* opposite Ben Affleck. And next up, she is Lady Penelope in TV series *Thunderbirds Are Go*.

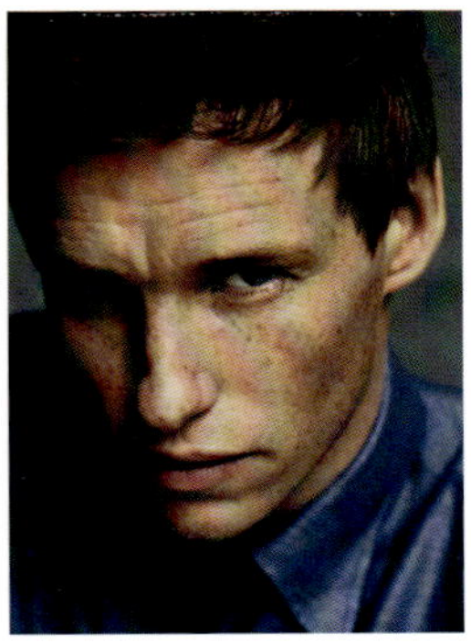

EDDIE REDMAYNE

Le Sirenuse, Positano, Italy

Winner of Academy, Golden Globe and BAFTA awards for his portrayal of Stephen Hawking in *The Theory of Everything*, Eddie Redmayne is well known both on stage and screen. He received a Tony for the Broadway production of *Red*, and he is also known for his roles in *Savage Grace*, *The Danish Girl* and *Fantastic Beasts and Where to Find Them*.

GUY RITCHIE

Soneva Fushi, Maldives

It was after watching *Butch Cassidy and the Sundance Kid* as a child that British director Guy Ritchie realised he wanted to make films for a living. He never attended film school, but got a job as a runner and worked his way up. His quirky gangster films *Lock, Stock and Two Smoking Barrels*, *Snatch* and *Revolver* have a cult following.

ELIE SAAB

Four Seasons Hotel George V, Paris, France

By the age of eight, fashion designer Elie Saab had already turned his attention to couture - he used to cut patterns out of newspaper, and, with his sister as a model, raid his mother's wardrobe for anything he could drape on her. Elie lives in Beirut and travels to Paris all the time. His favorite holiday destinations are the Maldives and Greece.

TABITHA SIMMONS

1 Hotel South Beach, Miami, United States

With a career that started in modelling, Tabitha Simmons launched her debut shoe collection in 2009. Her designs are inspired by her British roots and extensive travels around the world. 'I recently did a photoshoot in New Orleans and instantly fell in love with it, so am desperate to go back and explore it properly. I also adore Colombia.'

SIR PAUL SMITH

Claridge's, London, United Kingdom

After founding his company with a single shop in 1970, Paul Smith now has more than three hundred stores worldwide. He is renowned for his creative spirit and has been knighted for his services to British fashion. 'I call London home but am constantly on the go. In summer I try to slow down and spend some time with my wife, Pauline, in Tuscany.'

ALICE TEMPERLEY

Cheval Blanc Courchevel, France

A year after graduating from the Royal College of Art, Alice Temperley founded her fashion label Temperley London. Alice continues to head up the creative direction of the British brand, but when she's taking time out it's the beaches in Escondido, Mexico that she can't resist. 'They're the best in the world. I love the colours.'

STELLA TENNANT

Lismore Castle, Ireland

Raised on a sheep farm in northern England, model Stella Tennant was an art student hoping to pursue a career as a sculptor before she was discovered by the late Isabella Blow. Once based out of London and New York, she now lives with her husband and their four children in the Scottish countryside, where she spends time gardening and sculpting.

FLORENCE WELCH

Chateau Marmont, Los Angeles, United States

By the age of twenty-one, London-born Florence Welch had two international hit albums with her band Florence + the Machine. *Lungs* won the Brit Awards Album of the Year, and her second album, *Ceremonials*, was Grammy-nominated, which meant five years of back-to-back recording, promoting and touring. She lives in London but spends a lot of time in LA.

KATE WINSLET

Eilean Shona, Scotland

At the age of seventeen, Kate made an international name for herself in Peter Jackson's film *Heavenly Creatures*. She went on to be cast as Rose in James Cameron's *Titanic* opposite Leonardo DiCaprio. Kate won her first Academy Award for her role in *The Reader* and starred alongside Michael Fassbender in the Apple biopic *Steve Jobs*.

JASON WU

Hotel Esencia, Xpu-Há, Mexico

Having moved from Taiwan when he was nine, it was in Vancouver that Jason Wu learned how to sew, draft patterns and sketch in fashion proportions. These days his designs are worn by the likes of First Lady Michelle Obama, Julianne Moore and Christy Turlington Burns. Jason splits his time between Metzingen and Berlin, and his favourite holiday spots are Bali and Tulum.

PHOTOGRAPHERS

LUCAS ALLEN

Hotel Esencia; Grand Hotel a Villa Feltrinelli

Having started shooting professionally at twenty-one, Lucas Allen has had his personal work included in both solo and group exhibitions. His 2001 show *Les Pêcheurs d'Essaouira* featured his portraits of Moroccan fishermen and their environment. Originally from Melbourne, Lucas now splits his time between Australia and New York.

JAMES BEDFORD

Eilean Shona; Hôtel La Mamounia

London-based James Bedford has assisted photographers including Lord Snowdon. He now works with design agencies, hotels and restaurants as well as magazines. 'The most photogenic spot I know has to be Patagonia in autumn – truly the most amazing colours I've ever seen.'

MATTHEW BUCK

1 Hotel South Beach; The Carlyle; Claridge's; The Greenwich; Ham Yard Hotel; Palácio Belmonte; Suján Rajmahal Palace

Raised in Margate, Matthew Buck moved to London in the mid-1990s to work at Metro Studios in Clerkenwell as a studio assistant. He went on to spend five years at Paul Smith, installing the window displays in London, Paris and New York. Now Matthew is the photographic editor at *Condé Nast Traveller* and shoots regularly for the magazine as well as commissioning content.

JULIEN CAPMEIL

Six Senses Zighy Bay

As a child, Julien Capmeil stumbled across a box of his dad's underwater photos from the 1970s – images of a pristine barrier reef and neoprene-clad divers – and knew he had to be a photographer. He lives and works in Brooklyn and wonders when his son will find the box he just hid for him.

TIM EVAN-COOK

Cliveden House; Soho House Istanbul

Originally a fashion photographer, Tim Evan-Cook continued to pursue his love of movement by photographing boxers and dancers. He has lived in New York, Paris, Sydney and Milan but always returns to London, where he is now based with his wife, daughter, cat and dog.

ANDREA FAZZARI

Park Hyatt Tokyo

Before becoming a photographer, Andrea Fazzari worked in public relations for Dolce & Gabbana. She has lived in Manhattan, Paris, Florence, Hong Kong and now Tokyo, where she has quickly become an insider on the city's food scene. Andrea speaks French, Italian and Spanish and is studying Japanese.

SQUIRE FOX

Ace Hotel Portland; Hotel Esencia; One&Only Palmilla; Saint Cecilia

Known for his graphically arresting images, Squire Fox has his roots in the American South. His father and grandfathers were all bourbon-drinking furniture makers, and he moved seventeen times as a child. 'I've travelled all over, but New York is still my favourite city. The extremes, the energy and noises are like nowhere else.'

ALICE GAO

Four Seasons Hotel George V, Paris; Le Royal Monceau, Paris

Travel and still-life photographer Alice Gao considers her style to be modern, soulful and considered. 'Choosing a favourite place is a bit like asking someone to name their favourite child. I love Iceland and I just visited these amazing desert dunes a couple of hours outside of Abu Dhabi. But then, of course, there is always Paris.'

KEN KOCHEY

Parrot Cay; UXUA Casa Hotel & Spa

Based in New York, Ken Kochey regularly shoots for both editorial and commercial clients. But, he says, 'Rome resonates with me in a way that no other place ever has. I love wandering the back streets where the food, wine and architecture are unparalleled. I find the whole city irresistible.'

TOM PARKER

Ceylon Tea Trails

During the Asian tsunami in 2004, Tom Parker's career as a photographer was solidified as his pictures of the unfolding tragedy were used on the front pages of almost every international newspaper. He hasn't stopped travelling since. 'I've just discovered Santiago in Cuba. The spirit there makes Havana feel very wooden and conservative in comparison.'

BILL PHELPS

Lismore Castle

The co-designer and owner of Café Moto in Williamsburg, Brooklyn, Bill Phelps was born in Minnesota. He's picked up both an IPA Lucie Award and the Grand Prize of Portraits for the World Press. 'I saw Cocteau's *Beauty and the Beast* in Paris at the age of six, and it helped to set the stage for a lifetime of inspiration.'

OLIVER PILCHER

Le Sirenuse

Having studied sculpture at Edinburgh College of Art, Oliver Pilcher now lives and works in New York with his wife and four children. 'My favourite family holiday spot is Zahara de los Atunes in southern Spain. It's a beautiful Atlantic beach with white sand and warm blue waters.'

STEFANO SCATÀ

Aman Venice; Palazzo Margherita

Born in Pordenone, Stefano Scatà is a graduate of Italian literature and philosophy. He lives in Bassano del Grappa, specialising in interiors, food and travel. He feels most at home when on the island of Lampedusa in Sicily and in the south of Tyrol.

MICHAEL PAUL

La Colombe d'Or; Mandarin Oriental Bangkok; Song Saa

A keen skier, fly fisherman and cyclist, Michael Paul is based in London. 'My latest discovery is Yonaguni, one of the Yaeyama Islands in Japan. It's blessed with a tropical rainforest climate, fringed with pristine sandy beaches and has unbelievable diving.'

RICHARD POWERS

Chateau Marmont

Based in the south of France, British photographer Richard Powers works directly with architects, interior designers, hotels and a number of publishing houses, with thirteen coffee-table books to his name. 'I have spent many months of my life in India and Sri Lanka, where the light and colour is incredibly inspiring.'

JESSICA SAMPLE

Hotel Bel-Air

From a very young age, Jessica Sample travelled with her parents to Bhutan, Tibet, Africa and Indonesia with her camera in tow. Her favourite beach is Loon Point in Santa Barbara. 'The Mars-like rock formations are as good as the fish tacos at Padaro Beach Grill. And sometimes you can even see dolphins swim by.'

DANIEL WARD

Amilla Fushi

Beauty photographer Daniel Ward splits his time between London, Paris and Milan shooting editorial and advertising pictures for international clients. 'The most photogenic place I've ever shot must be Vang Vieng in Laos. Those beautiful limestone hills and the mist in the morning give the sense of viewing a painting.'

GREG WILLIAMS

Cheval Blanc Courchevel

Originally working behind the scenes on film franchises including James Bond, Greg Williams learned various techniques from many of the world's great cinematographers. He is also known for his portraits of stars, including Brad Pitt, Cate Blanchett, George Clooney and Robert De Niro.

MANOLO YLLERA

Aman Summer Palace

Spanish photographer Manolo Yllera was inspired by the work of Henri Cartier-Bresson and started taking pictures for fun. When he's not shooting, his perfect holiday is anywhere he can take his dogs. 'I love being in the countryside so that I can enjoy the silence and read lots of books.'

JENNY ZARINS

Soneva Fushi

Born in Sweden, Jenny Zarins is now based in London. There is a palpable sense of place across her work, be it travel, food or fashion. She loves Playa Guiones in Costa Rica, where, as a wannabe surfer, the waves keep her entertained.

WITH SPECIAL THANKS TO:

AMPERSAND TRAVEL

Specialising in luxury tailor-made travel to the Indian subcontinent, South-east Asia and the Far East, Ampersand creates journeys that fully engage the senses and constantly surprise and delight. From cultural tours of Central India to gastronomic adventures and dipping into the colourful markets of South-east Asia, the company helps you get under the skin of the destination, revealing its beauty in touching and unforgettable ways.

ampersandtravel.com
+44 20 7819 9770

THE BRAZILIAN BEACH HOUSE COMPANY

Dedicated to renting fully staffed private properties on the coast of Brazil, the Brazilian Beach House Company has an exclusive portfolio of about eighty astonishing properties. These include villas, beach houses and private islands. Everything is priced clearly by the night and the cost of extra services (transfers, boat charter, extra staff) are all transparent and upfront.

brazilianbeachhouse.com
+598 2605 6913

CLEVELAND COLLECTION

Luxury tour operator Cleveland Collection designs bespoke itineraries to some of the most exciting destinations worldwide. The combination of first-hand experience, in-depth destination knowledge and passion for travel means they have the expertise to recommend the perfect city break as well as a secluded beach escape in a private villa.

clevelandcollection.co.uk
+44 20 7843 3531

HEALING HOLIDAYS

A specialist spa and wellness company, Healing Holidays offers bespoke tailor-made trips to the world's best spas, retreats and medi-clinics. Having personally visited and extensively reviewed all properties and retreats, Healing Holidays only offers those at the top of their game and can pre-book all treatments as well as requesting the very best doctors, trainers and practitioners.

healingholidays.co.uk
+44 20 7843 3592

THE OXFORD SKI COMPANY

Luxury ski experts the Oxford Ski Company have more than seventeen years' experience in curating the finest ski holidays tailored to clients' individual requirements. They can recommend the best property match from their handpicked portfolio of over five hundred luxury chalets and hotels as well as organising the finer details of a trip from ski schools, childcare, activity bookings and private parties.

oxfordski.com
+44 20 8682 5000

SCOTT DUNN

As well as creating bespoke experiences and once-in-a-lifetime adventures, Scott Dunn also operates their own luxury ski chalets in the Alps and family villas in the Mediterranean sun, complete with Scott Dunn staff and private nannies. Their travel consultants each spend a month per year seeking out the best properties and fine-tuning their local knowledge so they can craft unique holidays for every client.

scottdunn.com
+44 20 3642 1194

CONTRIBUTOR PHOTO CREDITS

Tom Allen, Tom Beard, Tomo Brejk, Tom Craig, James Deacon, Patrick Demarchelier, Stephanie Diani, Simon Emmett, Garance Doré, Julian Hargreaves/LUZphoto/eyevine, Jonathan Hession, Johannes Huebl, James Mooney, Tom Munro, Dick Page & James Gibbs, Hal Shinnie, Johanne Shuebl

ACKNOWLEDGEMENTS

Assouline would like to thank Melinda, Fiona, Matthew and Tabitha at *Condé Nast Traveller* for their wonderful collaboration. Thanks also to Esther Kremer, Camille Dubois, Jihyun Kim, Lindsey Tulloch, Jackie Shao, Andrea Chlad, Cheryl Della Pietra and Justin O'Neill for their invaluable work on this book.

CREDITS